BEFORE WE MARRY

A JOURNAL FOR CHRISTIAN COUPLES

BEFORE WE MARRY

250 QUESTIONS FOR COUPLES TO GROW TOGETHER IN FAITH

Suzanne Shaw, PsyD, LMFT

ROCKRIDGE
PRESS

Copyright © 2022 by Rockridge Press

First Rockridge Press trade paperback edition 2022

Rockridge Press and the Rockridge Press logo are trademarks or registered trademarks of Callisto Media Inc. and/or its affiliates in the United States and other countries and may not be used without written permission.

For general information on our other products and services, please contact our Customer Care Department within the United States at (866) 744-2665, or outside the United States at (510) 253-0500.

Paperback ISBN: 978-1-68539-189-8

Manufactured in the United States of America

Interior and Cover Designer: Jill Lee
Art Producer: Maya Melenchuk
Editor: Brian Skulnik
Production Editor: Dylan Julian
Production Manager: Martin Worthington

Author photo courtesy of Gene Dalais of That's Fun Photography. All images used under license from Shutterstock.

10 9 8 7 6 5 4 3 2 1 0

This journal belongs to:

_____

_____

HOW TO USE THIS BOOK

Welcome to *Before We Marry*!

Maybe you recently got engaged, or maybe you just want to grow in your relationship in a fun, intentional way. Maybe you purchased this book for yourself, or maybe you received it as a gift. Either way, you're in for a treat with this questions-based couples journal. Each question serves as a springboard into reflections for yourselves as individuals and into conversations together. Written with Christian couples in mind, the questions aim to explore issues of faith alongside a variety of other topics to strengthen your relationship with each other and with God. You will learn a lot about your similarities and differences, and you'll gain a richer, deeper appreciation for each other as you discuss!

There are five broad categories:

 Family and Friends: These questions are about the relationships you have been born into as well as those you've chosen in your life, and how they have shaped your character and experience.

 Faith and Values: These questions focus on your belief in God as well as other beliefs, principles, and priorities that shape your ideals, actions, and decisions.

 You and Me: These questions focus on your relationship, its unique history, and how you can strengthen it together.

 Past, Present, and Future: These questions look at life through the perspective of time: share things from before you met, discuss what's important now, and shape the future you'd like to have together.

The World around Us: These questions explore broader subjects like culture, news, and geography, and focus on the many things you can do to have fun, grow, and make a meaningful contribution to the world.

There is a separate space underneath each question for both partners to jot down notes. There is also extra space in the back of this book if you need more writing room. Take turns writing, then share your notes with each other, sparking even more thoughts, questions, and conversations. Listen to your partner's answers with open-mindedness, curiosity, compassion, and emotional generosity. Make this a judgment-free, criticism-free zone so you both feel safe to open up and be known. You don't have to answer every single question or do them in any particular order. Have fun, and maybe even write some questions of your own!

Who was your best friend growing up? What is your favorite memory of them? Are you still in touch with them? If not, why?

How has your view of God changed in the past five years? What is the main thing you have learned about God's character since you became a believer?

When and where did you first see your partner and what was your first impression of them? Has that first impression proven to be true over time?

_____

_____

_____

_____

_____

_____

_____

If you could repeat one year of your life so far, which would it be and why? Which year would you never want to repeat?

_____

_____

_____

_____

_____

_____

_____

_____

How interested are you in what's happening in the stock market and the economy at large? What do you and your partner want to research or invest in financially?

How interested are you in what's happening in the stock market and the economy at large? What do you and your partner want to research or invest in financially?

What top three qualities do you look for in a good friend? Do you tend to have one best friend, a small group of intimate friends, or a larger network of different friends?

What is one of your favorite Christian or spirituality books? What is the main thing you learned from it? Are you reading any spirituality books right now? Which ones?

_____

_____

_____

_____

_____

_____

_____

What is something you admire about your partner? This could be a character trait, a goal they have achieved, an outlook they have, or a practice in their life.

_____

_____

_____

_____

_____

_____

_____

What is something you want more of in your life right now? What is something you want less of? Which of these things are within your control?

_____

_____

_____

_____

_____

_____

_____

Who is your favorite past or present U.S. president or world leader, and why? What do you consider to be good leadership qualities?

_____

_____

_____

_____

_____

_____

_____

What roles did you have in your family because of your gender or personality (e.g., the funny one, the caretaker, or the star)? How did you feel about having that role?

_____

_____

_____

_____

_____

_____

_____

What is an important virtue or character trait you are known for? Is it something you naturally possess or something you intentionally cultivated?

_____

_____

_____

_____

_____

_____

_____

What is something you need your partner to be especially patient or understanding about? What is one area in which you have a lot of patience or understanding for your partner?

_____

_____

_____

_____

_____

_____

_____

What is something you look forward to doing or learning in retirement? How does your faith shape your vision of what you will do in the future?

_____

_____

_____

_____

_____

_____

_____

_____

What is your favorite cuisine? What dishes do you especially like? Do you know how to make them? Would you take a cooking class to learn how?

When you were young, did you envision yourself having children? How about now? If the answer has changed, what caused it to change? Do you know if your partner wants children?

Which fruits of the Spirit (Galatians 5:22–23) do you demonstrate most in your life: love, joy, peace, patience, kindness, goodness, faithfulness, gentleness, or self-control? Which would you like to grow?

Rank the following love languages in order of greatest to least importance: physical touch, words of affirmation, gifts, acts of service, and quality time.

If you could have been born in any other time period in human history, what era would you choose? Is there a specific place you'd want to be? What attracts you to that time and place?

_____

_____

_____

_____

_____

_____

_____

_____

What issue do you see or read about in the news that especially stirs your empathy, anger, or passion? What actions have you taken to be more involved?

_____

_____

_____

_____

_____

_____

_____

_____

How do you feel about adoption? Does adoption change anything about your vision of parenthood? If so, what?

_____

_____

_____

_____

_____

_____

_____

What are your views on familial roles? Are you more traditional or contemporary? In what ways?

_____

_____

_____

_____

_____

_____

_____

What are your pet names, nicknames, or terms of endearment for each other? How did those names come about? What is your favorite way to be addressed by your partner?

Would you sign up to have your body cryogenically frozen to populate a new planet in the future? Why or why not? Would your faith influence this decision?

What is one feel-good, human-interest story you have read or heard about lately? What touched you about it?

Have you ever considered being a foster parent? What about this experience does or does not appeal to you? What are your preconceptions about foster children?

What qualities of a good leader do you think you and your partner have? If you are not already a leader, in what capacity can you envision yourself leading?

_____

_____

_____

_____

_____

_____

_____

_____

What is your favorite song? What is your partner's? What song makes you think of your relationship? What lyrics can you think of that describe your feelings for your partner?

_____

_____

_____

_____

_____

_____

_____

_____

If you could go back in time, what's one thing you would change or do differently in your life? Why?

How many of the fifty states have you been to? How many countries? Where is your favorite place to visit? Where would you like to go next?

What would you enjoy most about being a godparent or guardian to other people's children? How do you feel about babysitting other people's children? For how long?

Describe your relationship or experiences with different aspects of God: the Father, the Son (Jesus), and the Holy Spirit? What images, feelings, or memories does each bring up?

What new traditions, rituals, or celebrations have you created as a couple? If you don't have any yet, are there any you'd like to try?

_____

_____

_____

_____

_____

_____

_____

You may have heard that your spirituality and mental health both benefit from "being present." Is that easy or difficult for you to do? If it's difficult, what's the main challenge you encounter?

_____

_____

_____

_____

_____

_____

_____

What is your opinion about professional sports? What teams or players do you follow, if any? What qualities do you admire in an athlete?

_____

_____

_____

_____

_____

_____

_____

How comfortable do you feel asking other people to watch your children or pets? Would you only trust family? What about friends or people from church, work, or a job website?

_____

_____

_____

_____

_____

_____

_____

How often do you usually pray? Is your prayer style casual and conversational or more formal and structured? When do you like to pray?

_____

_____

_____

_____

_____

_____

_____

If you had an unlimited amount of money, what's something you'd like to do for or give to your partner to surprise them for their birthday or your anniversary?

_____

_____

_____

_____

_____

_____

_____

Do you have a bucket list? If so, what are some of the items on your list? Are there any you've already done?

_____

_____

_____

_____

_____

_____

_____

What is a culture in the world that interests you? How did you become interested in that culture? What have you done to learn more about it?

_____

_____

_____

_____

_____

_____

_____

What is your ideal family plan? If you want children, how do you feel about having kids before or outside of marriage? How important is it to you to make this decision before you are married?

_____

_____

_____

_____

_____

_____

_____

Write down a Bible verse that's been especially meaningful or powerful in your life. When and why did the verse become important to you?

_____

_____

_____

_____

_____

_____

_____

A "total marriage" is a marriage in which the couple does almost everything together, including sharing work, friendships, and hobbies. What are your thoughts and feelings about this type of marriage?

_____

_____

_____

_____

_____

_____

_____

Some people may focus more on the past, present, or future. Which of these do you tend to focus on? How does that affect your relationship?

_____

_____

_____

_____

_____

_____

_____

Do you enjoy watching the Olympics? What are your favorite sports to watch in the Games? If the Olympics aren't your thing, what other live events do you like to tune in for?

_____

_____

_____

_____

_____

_____

What are your most important values when it comes to parenting? What would be the most important lessons to teach your kids? How does faith play a role?

_____

_____

_____

_____

_____

_____

_____

What are your beliefs about tithing, or giving 10 percent of your income to a church or Christian cause? Will you tithe as a couple? Why or why not?

Consider these three purposes of money: Enjoy your life, save for the future, and give to others. Which of these most reflects your attitude on financial matters? How about your partner?

When you think about how you spend your time, what is the most productive thing you do in your day or week? What activity or habit is your biggest time waster?

_____

_____

_____

_____

_____

_____

_____

What is the first concert or live music performance you ever went to as an adult? Do you listen to any live performances on repeat? What bands or artists are your favorites?

_____

_____

_____

_____

_____

_____

_____

What do you appreciate most about the way you were raised? What were your parents' or guardians' strengths? How would you like to emulate them, and what would you do differently?

_____

_____

_____

_____

_____

_____

_____

What is the most important thing you spend money on? What is something you'd like to spend less on? How does your faith influence how you use your money?

_____

_____

_____

_____

_____

_____

_____

What are your favorite features of your partner's body? How do you feel about the level of physical affection between you? What part of the body do you most enjoy having your partner touch?

What was the best job you've ever had? Why? What is the worst job you've ever had? Why? What did you learn from each of these jobs?

What do you think is the greatest invention in human history? If you could invent anything, what would it be? How would it benefit humanity?

_____

_____

_____

_____

_____

_____

_____

How do you feel about higher education, sports, music, art, and religion in bringing up your child? Which are important, and which are optional? What else is important?

_____

_____

_____

_____

_____

_____

_____

What would you say to or do for someone who struggles to believe that God exists or that God is good because of all the evil and suffering they see in the world?

_____

_____

_____

_____

_____

_____

_____

What is one thing you and your partner like or feel exactly the same way about? What is one thing you have wildly different tastes or opinions about?

_____

_____

_____

_____

_____

_____

_____

If you could be a famous person in world history, who would you choose to be and why? Who do you think your partner would choose to be? Why?

_____

_____

_____

_____

_____

_____

_____

Briefly describe your level of involvement or activism in politics. How much do you believe in the ability of political parties, candidates, or offices to change things on a local or national level?

_____

_____

_____

_____

_____

_____

_____

When you were young, were you a member of a social organization such as a church youth group? If so, how did it shape you? Share a favorite memory.

1 Corinthians 12:8–10 lists service, wisdom, knowledge, faith, healing, miracle-working, prophecy, spiritual discernment, and tongues as spiritual gifts. Which of these do you most see in yourself?

Is there a movie, play, poem, song, painting, or book that best represents the essence of your relationship? What is it, and why?

_____

_____

_____

_____

_____

_____

_____

_____

What is a small habit you can begin (individually or together) that you will be glad you started a year from now?

_____

_____

_____

_____

_____

_____

_____

_____

How environmentally conscious are you? What conservation measures do you take in your life? Some possible examples include owning an electric car, recycling, eating organic or vegan, installing solar panels, and bicycling.

_____

_____

_____

_____

_____

_____

_____

John 15:13 says, "Greater love has no one than this: to lay down one's life for one's friends." Is there anyone you would be willing to die for? Under what circumstances?

_____

_____

_____

_____

_____

_____

_____

In Matthew 25:40, Jesus says, "Whatever you did for one of the least of these brothers and sisters of mine, you did for me." Who are the "least of these"? What's something you've done for them?

_____

_____

_____

_____

_____

_____

What is your idea of a perfect Friday night? What is your partner's? How do you negotiate if you have different ideas?

_____

_____

_____

_____

_____

_____

_____

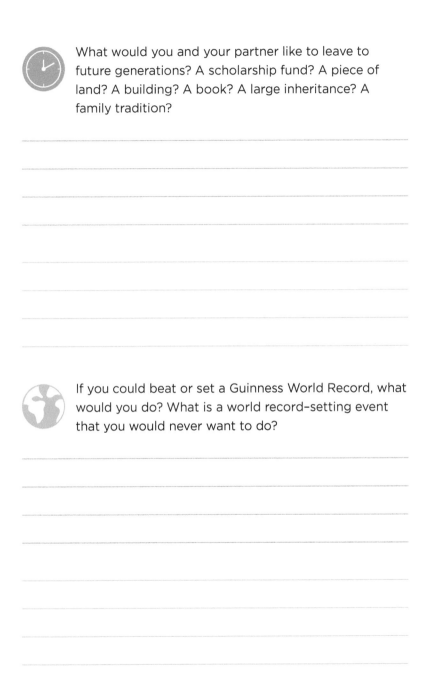

What would you and your partner like to leave to future generations? A scholarship fund? A piece of land? A building? A book? A large inheritance? A family tradition?

If you could beat or set a Guinness World Record, what would you do? What is a world record–setting event that you would never want to do?

Who is the most influential person you know? What do you love, admire, or appreciate most about them? What do you think is the best thing you've learned from knowing them?

What is the most important thing for a couple to agree on or have the same worldview about? What's the least important?

How do you feel when your partner wants alone time? What about when they want to do something with their friends? What do you enjoy doing with your alone time?

_____

_____

_____

_____

_____

_____

_____

It is often noted that couples can grow to look, talk, dress, or act similarly over time. In what ways do you hope to become more like your partner over time?

_____

_____

_____

_____

_____

_____

_____

_____

How adventurous are you? What's the scariest or most exciting thing you've ever done? What's something beyond your comfort zone you'd like to try someday?

Who is the most influential person you've never met? They can be an author, a celebrity, or someone else. What is the best thing you've learned from them?

What was one of your most memorable or significant answered prayers? How long did you pray for it? What do you pray for the most?

_____

_____

_____

_____

_____

_____

_____

_____

What feelings do you have about your sexuality and your past sexual experiences? What feelings do you have when you anticipate a sexual future with your partner?

_____

_____

_____

_____

_____

_____

_____

_____

How has your sexuality changed over the course of your lifetime? Are there ways you would like to grow in that area in the future?

_____

_____

_____

_____

_____

_____

_____

What cartoons, comic strips, comic books, or animated movies did you like as a child? Are there any you still enjoy as an adult?

_____

_____

_____

_____

_____

_____

_____

Who was an important adult in your childhood besides a parent or guardian (e.g., a relative, teacher, coach, or pastor)? What were they like? How did they impact you?

What has been one of your unanswered prayers? How do you deal with prayers that are not answered in the way you would have hoped?

What pattern, if any, do you see in the kind of people you were attracted to or dated in the past? Does your current partner fit that pattern?

_____

_____

_____

_____

_____

_____

_____

What was going on in your mother's life when she was pregnant with you? Are you aware of any special issues or circumstances around your conception and birth?

_____

_____

_____

_____

_____

_____

_____

What languages have you learned or tried to learn? What new language would you like to speak if it came easily to you?

_____

_____

_____

_____

_____

_____

_____

_____

Did you grow up with pets? What was your relationship with them like? If they died, how did you handle that loss?

_____

_____

_____

_____

_____

_____

_____

_____

Is it morally wrong to eat any particular kinds of food? How about consuming different forms of art like movies, books, or TV? Are any of these off-limits for you?

_____

_____

_____

_____

_____

_____

_____

Genesis 2:24 says when a couple marries they separate from their original families and "become one flesh." What does this mean to you? Do you think this defines the bond of marriage accurately?

_____

_____

_____

_____

_____

_____

_____

Do you feel that you have plenty of time, just enough time, or not enough time to do what you'd like? Consider a day, a week, a year, and a lifetime.

What is your attitude toward and experience of poverty? Tell of a time you lived in, saw, or were aware of poverty. How did it affect you?

What role do animals play in your life? Do you consider yourself to be an animal lover? If so, what does that look like?

_____

_____

_____

_____

_____

_____

_____

Acts 20:35 says, "It is more blessed to give than to receive." What does this mean to you? How generous are you? How generous is your partner? In what ways?

_____

_____

_____

_____

_____

_____

_____

How important to you is your image or personal style, such as the way you dress or do your hair? What do you like best about your partner's clothing style or hairstyle?

_____

_____

_____

_____

_____

_____

_____

What is one thing you feel takes too much of your time? Conversely, what is one thing you'd like to spend more time doing?

_____

_____

_____

_____

_____

_____

_____

How do you feel about war? Do you believe there are just wars? If you do, what does that mean to you? How does your faith influence your views?

_____

_____

_____

_____

_____

_____

_____

When you were growing up, what did you feel you were supposed to be or do (e.g., smart, productive, or nice) to be a good member of your family? Do you still have those values?

_____

_____

_____

_____

_____

_____

_____

In Mark 10:27, Jesus explains the concept of miracles: "With man this is impossible, but not with God; all things are possible with God." Describe a miracle you've experienced.

_____

_____

_____

_____

_____

_____

_____

_____

Can you think of a time your partner stuck up for you or defended you somehow? What was it about? How did that make you feel?

_____

_____

_____

_____

_____

_____

_____

_____

Was there a time in your past when you felt your life was protected or saved, either by someone else or by God? How do you feel when you think about that?

_____

_____

_____

_____

_____

_____

_____

For years, _British GQ_ magazine has published a list of "the 100 best things in the world." What would be the top items on your own list of the best things in the world?

_____

_____

_____

_____

_____

_____

_____

When you were growing up, what did you feel you were not supposed to do or be (e.g., lazy, cheap, or wasteful) to be a good member of your family? Do you do any of those things now?

What do you believe about the possibility of life on planets other than Earth? What do you believe about UFOs? Ghosts? How do you explain paranormal activity?

What is your experience or assessment of your sexual drive? Do you feel it is high, average, or low? What about your partner's?

_____

_____

_____

_____

_____

_____

_____

What are you most thankful for in your life right now that you haven't had in the past? Did you work to get this, or was it a gift?

_____

_____

_____

_____

_____

_____

_____

How do you feel about amusement parks? What do you like or dislike about them?

_____

_____

_____

_____

_____

_____

_____

_____

Which of your values as an adult did you learn growing up? Which have you modified, grown out of, or otherwise discarded to be your own person?

_____

_____

_____

_____

_____

_____

_____

_____

What have you grown up learning about gratitude, appreciation, and thankfulness? Were you taught to express appreciation or write thank-you notes?

_____

_____

_____

_____

_____

_____

_____

_____

As a couple, how will you navigate times when your sexual desires don't align?

_____

_____

_____

_____

_____

_____

_____

_____

Imagine your funeral. What would you like people to say about you and your life? What would you like written on your gravestone?

_____

_____

_____

_____

_____

_____

Have you ever taken a world history class or read a world history book? If so, what struck you most about it? Do you think history repeats itself?

_____

_____

_____

_____

_____

_____

What number child are you in the birth order of your family? How do you think this has influenced you and your relationships?

What do you think are the most important practices for being healthy? What are your best health practices and what do you need help to improve upon?

What are your feelings and ideas about being a working parent? A stay-at-home parent? Would either you or your partner like to be the primary caretaker of your kids?

What is your ideal life span? What do you think is the best way to pass on? How do you feel about making end-of-life plans? And when should you start?

What part of the world do you know the most about? What part of the world do you know the least about? Do you have a practice of reading world news?

_____

_____

_____

_____

_____

_____

_____

Did you have a small, medium, or large family (either nuclear or extended)? How has this influenced the family size you want to have?

_____

_____

_____

_____

_____

_____

_____

What are your feelings and experiences about reading or studying the Bible? What questions do you have about the Bible? Do you have a favorite book in the Bible?

_____

_____

_____

_____

_____

_____

_____

What spiritual practices do you want to incorporate into your relationship or marriage? How often? Give a concrete example, such as "join a weekly Bible study" or "pray together every night."

_____

_____

_____

_____

_____

_____

_____

What are your beliefs about "the end times"? Do you think they are coming soon? What do you think will happen? Do you do anything in your life to prepare for this?

How do you feel about the possibility of moving to another country? Where would you consider living, and for how long?

Did your parents or guardians model having a best friend or a group of friends? How often did your family participate in social events, parties, or spending time with another family or friends?

_____

_____

_____

_____

_____

_____

_____

What do you know about fasting, both from a nutritional and spiritual point of view? Why do you think Jesus encouraged his disciples to fast?

_____

_____

_____

_____

_____

_____

_____

Is there a cause or a group that you would like to help as a couple? What charities do you want to donate time or money to?

_____

_____

_____

_____

_____

_____

_____

What is something that helps you let go of the past? What is something that helps you not worry about the future? What helps you focus and be attentive in the present moment?

_____

_____

_____

_____

_____

_____

_____

How do you maintain or cultivate hope when you see all the bad things happening in the news? Where do you look for encouragement, optimism, reassurance, or comfort?

Is *home* a place of refuge and privacy or a place of hospitality, activity, and people to you? What does home mean to your partner?

Do you believe spiritual transformation is organic or more intentional? What are you doing that you would consider a spiritually transformational practice?

_____

_____

_____

_____

_____

_____

_____

_____

What ideas come to mind when you encounter the word *romantic*? How romantic do you consider your-self to be? What is the most romantic moment you have shared with your partner?

_____

_____

_____

_____

_____

_____

_____

_____

What things do you expect to decrease the longer you are together in this relationship? What things do you expect to increase?

_____

_____

_____

_____

_____

_____

_____

_____

If you could wave a magic wand and have one major world problem disappear immediately, what would it be? Why did you pick that one?

_____

_____

_____

_____

_____

_____

_____

_____

Did you have any older siblings growing up? If so, what did that teach you? If not, was there anyone else in your life who filled that role?

How do you feel about military spending? Do you value a strong military, or do you feel government money should be primarily spent on social services?

When married, will you and your partner keep separate bank accounts, have a joint bank account, or both? Will you consult each other before making purchases?

_____

_____

_____

_____

_____

_____

_____

When in your life were you in the best shape? What kind of activity or exercise were you doing at the time? How did that feel?

_____

_____

_____

_____

_____

_____

_____

How worried are you about climate change or global warming? What do you think humanity needs to do about it? How hopeful are you that serious changes can actually be made?

Did you have any younger siblings growing up? If so, what did that teach you? If not, was there anyone else in your life who filled that role?

What are your values around work? Do you try to put work first or achieve a work-life balance? Is there another phrase that captures your philosophy of work?

_____

_____

_____

_____

_____

_____

_____

How would you rate your and your partner's cleanliness on a scale from 1 to 10, with 1 being very messy and 10 being extremely neat? How will you deal with differences in how clean you keep your living area?

_____

_____

_____

_____

_____

_____

_____

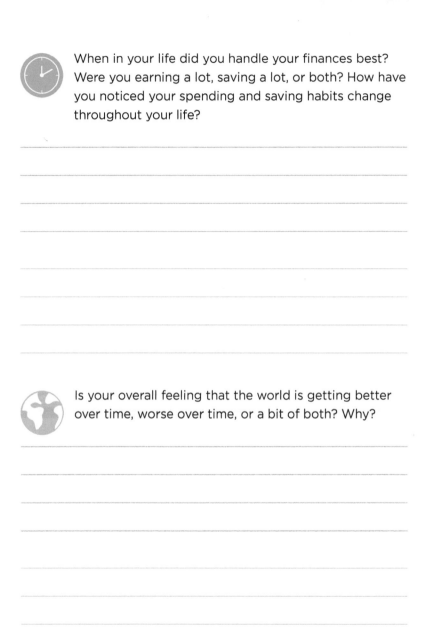

When in your life did you handle your finances best? Were you earning a lot, saving a lot, or both? How have you noticed your spending and saving habits change throughout your life?

Is your overall feeling that the world is getting better over time, worse over time, or a bit of both? Why?

How are you similar to and different from your sibling(s)? If you have several siblings, choose one or two. If you are an only child, have you ever wanted a sibling?

_____

_____

_____

_____

_____

_____

_____

What are your feelings about waste? How conscientious are you when it comes to conserving (i.e., not wasting) money, food, electricity, gas, time, or other resources?

_____

_____

_____

_____

_____

_____

_____

What kinds of fun activities do you enjoy doing together? Tell your partner about one of the most fun times you ever shared with them.

_____

_____

_____

_____

_____

_____

_____

How many habits do you have that are helping you work toward a future goal? What are they? How is the progress toward your goal coming along?

_____

_____

_____

_____

_____

_____

_____

_____

How do you interpret the juxtaposition of John 3:16 ("For God so loved the world that He gave His one and only Son") with 1 John 2:15 ("Do not love the world or anything in the world")?

_____

_____

_____

_____

_____

_____

_____

Did your parents or guardians let you sleep over at friends' houses? Was there somewhere else you slept overnight? How did you feel being away from home? Would you allow your child to do that?

_____

_____

_____

_____

_____

_____

_____

Do you think children should be given chores? If so, what kind of chores? Should they be given an allowance? If so, should it be based on chores or not? Why?

_____

_____

_____

_____

_____

_____

_____

As a couple, do you want to have a descriptive budget (keeping track of spending) or a prescriptive budget (limiting amounts in each category)? What feelings come up around budgeting?

_____

_____

_____

_____

_____

_____

_____

What have you noticed yourself gaining or losing as you grow older? Do you feel a trade-off of youth and energy for maturity and wisdom? What other trade-offs are happening?

_____

_____

_____

_____

_____

_____

_____

What do you think is the healthiest use of social media? If you have ever taken a break from social media, what feelings came up?

_____

_____

_____

_____

_____

_____

_____

Psalm 68:6 says, "God sets the lonely in families." When have you felt lonely? Did God provide you a place of belonging? What impact did that have on you?

What do you believe about the relationships among physical health and nutrition, sleep, exercise, social connectedness, faith, mindset, stress, and the environment? Rank each of these factors in order of importance to you.

Do you value waking up at the same time as your partner? Going to sleep at the same time? How similar or different are your circadian rhythms?

_____

_____

_____

_____

_____

_____

_____

What was your most memorable birthday? Who was there? If it had a theme, what was it? Do you tend to like celebrating your birthday?

_____

_____

_____

_____

_____

_____

_____

Have you ever, or would you ever, serve in your country's military forces? Which branch? How is that decision influenced by your faith?

_____

_____

_____

_____

_____

_____

_____

What ideas did you form or inherit from your upbringing (e.g., family, friends, culture, or faith) about masculinity and what men "should" be like? What about femininity and what women "should" be like?

_____

_____

_____

_____

_____

_____

_____

What is your experience with traditional medicine versus alternative healing methods and techniques? In your own health and wellness journey, what have you tried that has worked, and what hasn't?

What is something you think about frequently that your partner might not be aware of? How do you think they would react to discovering this?

What is something you received from someone that you have paid forward to someone else? What is something you have paid back? How did that feel?

_____

_____

_____

_____

_____

_____

_____

If you could suddenly be competent at any skill without having to practice, what would it be? Is there someone you know who has that skill?

_____

_____

_____

_____

_____

_____

_____

_____

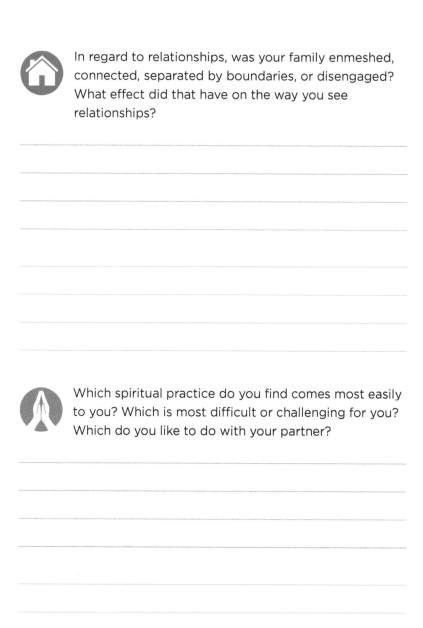

In regard to relationships, was your family enmeshed, connected, separated by boundaries, or disengaged? What effect did that have on the way you see relationships?

Which spiritual practice do you find comes most easily to you? Which is most difficult or challenging for you? Which do you like to do with your partner?

How would you feel about having an only child? How would you feel if you had twins or triplets? How would you feel about having someone—a family member or otherwise—provide live-in childcare help?

_____

_____

_____

_____

_____

_____

_____

What are your financial goals? Do you want to make a certain income, pay off debt, save up for a house, build your retirement fund, or something else?

_____

_____

_____

_____

_____

_____

_____

If you could play any musical instrument in the world, which one would it be? Would you play solo or in a band, worship team, or orchestra?

What was the role of music and dancing in your upbringing? How much expressive activity (e.g., making noise, making a mess, or moving your body) was allowed or encouraged growing up?

1 Corinthians 10:13 teaches that God will not let you be tempted beyond what you can bear. How do you deal with temptation in your life?

_____

_____

_____

_____

_____

_____

_____

What superpower would you like to have? What's one natural power that you already possess? What superpower could you see in your partner? And what natural power do they possess?

_____

_____

_____

_____

_____

_____

_____

If you could sit down with any famous historical figure for a one-on-one lunch, who would it be? What would you like to talk about with them?

_____

_____

_____

_____

_____

_____

_____

If you could be any animal in the world, which would you be? Why? What aspect of God's character does that animal demonstrate?

_____

_____

_____

_____

_____

_____

_____

_____

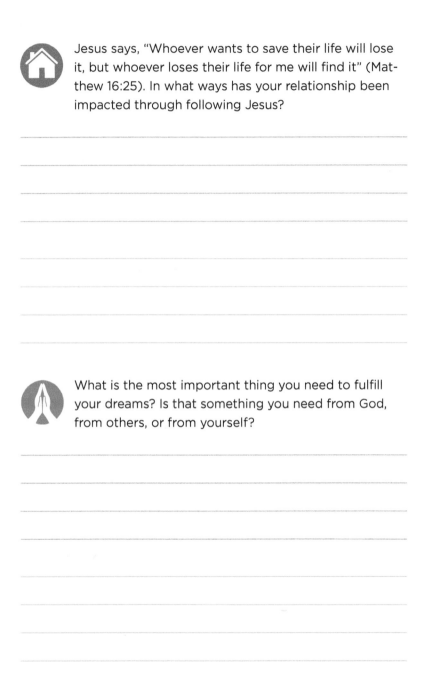

Jesus says, "Whoever wants to save their life will lose it, but whoever loses their life for me will find it" (Matthew 16:25). In what ways has your relationship been impacted through following Jesus?

What is the most important thing you need to fulfill your dreams? Is that something you need from God, from others, or from yourself?

What do you see more easily in your partner than they see in themselves? What do they see in you more easily than you see in yourself?

_____

_____

_____

_____

_____

_____

_____

When you were a child, what did you say you wanted to be when you grew up? Is that still true? If not, when did it change?

_____

_____

_____

_____

_____

_____

_____

What do you think is the most important scientific discovery of the last century? What issue do you think needs more focus or funding in scientific research?

_____

_____

_____

_____

_____

_____

_____

What is your ethnic or genetic heritage? How do you feel about being part of that group? Do you have pride, apprehension, confusion, curiosity, or any other emotions about your heritage?

_____

_____

_____

_____

_____

_____

_____

If you could start a nonprofit organization or charity, what would it be focused on? Who would it serve? What would you name it?

_____

_____

_____

_____

_____

_____

_____

Is it important to you to eat meals together with your partner? If so, which ones? How often? Do you prefer eating in or dining out?

_____

_____

_____

_____

_____

_____

_____

What do you think heaven is like? What are your feelings about going there and being there forever?

_____

_____

_____

_____

_____

_____

_____

What is your attitude toward and experience of luxury or wealth? When is a time you lived in, saw, or were exposed to luxurious living? How did it affect you?

_____

_____

_____

_____

_____

_____

_____

Is it possible to put too much importance on good things, like family, education, or health? Do you gravitate more toward the idea of a *balanced* life or a *passionate* life?

Which person in the Bible resonates with you the most? What traits do you share with them? If you could meet a biblical figure in person, who would it be?

What's one affirmation or compliment your partner has given you that meant a lot to you? What's the most meaningful compliment you can imagine giving?

What would you want to eat if you knew it was your last meal? Who would you want to eat it with? What would you talk about over the meal?

Which one of your available senses do you value and enjoy the most? Give an example of one thing you love experiencing with that sense.

_____

_____

_____

_____

_____

_____

_____

How do you feel about homeschooling? Were you homeschooled, and, if so, what was that experience like? Would you want to homeschool your children?

_____

_____

_____

_____

_____

_____

_____

What's one thing you know from your field of work or study that you might take for granted—something that people outside of your field might not even think about?

_____

_____

_____

_____

_____

_____

_____

What's something you didn't get to hear enough growing up that you would like your partner to tell you regularly? What words would be healing to your heart?

_____

_____

_____

_____

_____

_____

_____

_____

What's something you remember about fourth grade?
Who was your teacher? Who was your best friend?
What did you like to do at recess?

_____

_____

_____

_____

_____

_____

_____

If you could become the world's foremost expert on
any question or topic, what would it be? How broad or
narrow would your topic of expertise be?

_____

_____

_____

_____

_____

_____

_____

When you were growing up, how often did your family laugh together? What was the role of humor in your family? What is one funny story from your upbringing that you remember?

_____

_____

_____

_____

_____

_____

_____

Do you believe parents have an obligation to take care of their children at any age? If not, at what age are kids responsible for themselves?

_____

_____

_____

_____

_____

_____

_____

How do you feel about being taken care of when you are sick or hurt? How do you feel about taking care of your partner when they are sick or hurt?

_____

_____

_____

_____

_____

_____

_____

Who is an elderly person in your life that you want to be like when you grow older? What do you admire most about them?

_____

_____

_____

_____

_____

_____

_____

What subject matter or field of study do you find most fascinating? How did you discover your interest in it? Did you have a teacher or role model?

_____

_____

_____

_____

_____

_____

_____

How were you disciplined when you were a child? Were your parents or guardians more strict or permissive? What lessons did you learn as a result of the discipline you received?

_____

_____

_____

_____

_____

_____

_____

What promises have you made to yourself that you have kept? What promises have you made to yourself that you have broken? Do you need to forgive yourself?

_____

_____

_____

_____

_____

_____

_____

Is it easier for you to ask forgiveness from your partner or to forgive your partner? Is it easier for you to forgive your partner or to forgive yourself?

_____

_____

_____

_____

_____

_____

_____

Have you achieved your educational goals? If not, what other degrees, trainings, certifications, or licenses would you like to attain?

_____

_____

_____

_____

_____

_____

_____

If you could win any prestigious award in the world, which one would it be and what would it be for? Tell your partner why this award would be meaningful to you.

_____

_____

_____

_____

_____

_____

_____

How many times did you move before the age of eighteen? How do you think not moving much (stability) or moving a lot (mobility) affected you?

_____

_____

_____

_____

_____

_____

_____

What are your feelings about interpersonal conflict? Do you try to prevent or avoid conflict? When conflict happens, how do you resolve it?

_____

_____

_____

_____

_____

_____

_____

_____

What is your dream vacation? Do you like to stay home or travel? Do you prefer going to a new place or returning to a favorite place?

_____

_____

_____

_____

_____

_____

_____

What do you know now that you wish you knew ten years ago? If you had known this ten years ago, how do you imagine your life would be different?

_____

_____

_____

_____

_____

_____

_____

_____

Do you have a favorite hobby associated with travel or world discovery (e.g., studying maps, watching foreign movies, or reading books about other countries and cultures)? How could you enjoy this hobby as a couple?

As an adult, how easy or hard is it for you to make new friends? What helps you when meeting new people? How can your partner support you?

Do you believe joy is an inborn trait, learned through experience, or based on circumstances? Can joy be cultivated intentionally? If so, how?

What is something your partner does or could do to help you feel more confident, comfortable, or supported in social situations such as parties, holidays, or reunions?

Have you ever had a moment when you felt like time stood still? Describe what that was like. What was happening in that moment? Where was God in that moment?

_____

_____

_____

_____

_____

_____

_____

How patriotic are you? Do you know your national anthem by heart? Do you own a flag? Describe your feelings about your country. Does your partner feel similarly?

_____

_____

_____

_____

_____

_____

_____

How important to you is maintaining close relationships or frequent visits with your extended family? Any relatives in particular? How do you feel about your partner's extended family?

_____

_____

_____

_____

_____

_____

_____

Comment on the phrase "What goes around, comes around." Do you believe you get back in life what you put out? Do you believe people get what they deserve?

_____

_____

_____

_____

_____

_____

_____

_____

What is something your partner has introduced you to or made you aware of about yourself, the world, or God?

What is your favorite thing to do to kill time? What is something you do that makes the hours fly by like minutes?

What is your favorite mode of transportation? Why? What is a mode of transportation you have never tried? Would you and your partner like to try it together?

_____

_____

_____

_____

_____

_____

_____

What is the role of church, a small group, a recovery program, or another form of community in your faith or spirituality? Do you and your partner attend one together?

_____

_____

_____

_____

_____

_____

_____

Romans 12:13 says, "Practice hospitality." What was your parents' or guardians' attitude about opening their home to others? What are your feelings and ideas about hospitality as a couple?

_____

_____

_____

_____

_____

_____

_____

What's something your partner does or says that makes you feel safe and secure? This could be physical, emotional, financial, or something else.

_____

_____

_____

_____

_____

_____

_____

Do you look forward to becoming a grandparent? How involved do you imagine you would be in your grandkids' lives? What's one thing you'd like to do with them?

What are your thoughts about the legal ages for drinking, smoking, voting, serving in the military, and getting a driver's license? Would you change any of these ages? Why or why not?

If each person is a part of Christ's body, which body part are you? Which part is your partner? What do you appreciate about their part?

_____

_____

_____

_____

_____

_____

_____

_____

What do you believe about angels? Have you ever seen one or had an experience with one? If so, describe the experience.

_____

_____

_____

_____

_____

_____

_____

_____

What are your feelings about shopping? When is shopping fun for you, and when does shopping feel like a chore? How does your faith influence what you buy?

What are your favorite major and minor holidays? Do you have a favorite religious holiday? Secular holiday? Why?

What is one thing that could suddenly disappear in the world without making any difference to you whatsoever? Would its disappearance affect your partner?

Who is someone you usually have fun with or who makes you laugh? Who encourages you? Who inspires you? Who brings out your best self?

What is something you feel is worth doing well? What is something you don't mind doing poorly?

_____

_____

_____

_____

_____

_____

_____

Look up your Myers-Briggs personality type. Which categories (E/I, N/S, T/F, P/J) do you share with your partner? Which represent your biggest difference?

_____

_____

_____

_____

_____

_____

_____

Have you ever witnessed a birth? Have you ever witnessed a death? If so, how did those events impact you? Did they change your view of life or of God?

_____

_____

_____

_____

_____

_____

_____

What is the most beautiful kind of scenery to you? Where have you seen it? What do you feel about God when you witness it?

_____

_____

_____

_____

_____

_____

_____

What do you feel comfortable relying on others for? What do you prefer to do yourself? Would you like to rely more on others, or be more independent?

_____

_____

_____

_____

_____

_____

_____

_____

Do you believe in infant baptism, or do you prefer conscious consent? If you have been baptized, what age were you? Have you been baptized more than once?

_____

_____

_____

_____

_____

_____

_____

_____

Do you share secret looks, code words, or hand gestures as a couple that no one else understands? What are they?

What is your attitude about aging? Who do you know who has aged gracefully? Why do you think people fight aging so much? Why do you think our culture values youthfulness so much?

What traits (e.g., hard work, perseverance, or wisdom) do you notice in highly successful people? What traits do you think are responsible for your success? What role does faith play?

_____

_____

_____

_____

_____

_____

_____

What have you been taught about apologizing and taking responsibility for your mistakes and wrong-doings? How has this affected your relationships?

_____

_____

_____

_____

_____

_____

_____

What do you believe about the roles of pain, suffering, and struggle in life? Are they bad, good, or necessary? How does your faith shape your views about them?

Which of the two of you is a better driver? A better dishwasher? A better cook? A better dresser? A better singer? Has nicer handwriting? Tells better jokes?

If you could make only one significant change in your life, what would it be?

If you could distribute one thing to everyone in the world who needs it, what would it be? How do you think that thing would change peoples' lives?

Is there something that people have told you again and again throughout your life that you have a hard time believing? Why is it so hard to believe?

If you could take on someone else's problem or pain so they wouldn't have to deal with it, would you? Why or why not?

What things are you and your partner competitive about? Is it serious and intense or fun and lighthearted? What things are you more collaborative about?

_____

_____

_____

_____

_____

_____

_____

_____

Name something you would like to do every single day this year. Name something you'd like to do once a week, once a month, and once a year.

_____

_____

_____

_____

_____

_____

_____

_____

If you were God, what would be your next mission in the world? Where do you see God working in the world and in your life right now?

_____

_____

_____

_____

_____

_____

_____

Who is someone in your life you would like to share your faith with more? Who is someone you know that seems open to God or spiritual conversations?

_____

_____

_____

_____

_____

_____

_____

Have you had an experience of the kindness of God leading to repentance (Romans 2:4)? What does the idea of repentance bring up for you?

_____

_____

_____

_____

_____

_____

_____

_____

How does your partner make you a better person? What are some ways you have changed since you met them? How have they changed?

_____

_____

_____

_____

_____

_____

_____

_____

What are some of the most significant things you have learned about your partner and yourself in the process of completing this journal?

How is marriage—in general and in yours specifically—designed and intended to bless the people in your community and the world?

NOTES